KV-370-629

Like Keats, Erin Halliday launches herself into a poetic career in which a concept of poetry is not first and foremost a manner of writing but a manner of reading, of transforming what one had read into a way of life. Steeped in classical myth and Anglo-Saxon lore, using words as esoteric as gynandromorphic or glossarist, she twists Latin and Greek sources under a Hellenistic 'lens shift on the coppery gods' of Belfast and Down.

– Medbh McGuckian

Erin Halliday's poetry glitters with the bright abundant stock of the world, extravagant riches captured by a mind delighted with living things, and displayed in language that is coloured and transformative. History and myth contribute their surprises, classical skills are deployed, sometimes discreetly, sometimes with sheer delight in performance. In her own phrase, what she shows the reader is 'a courtship of angles', a dazzle of perspectives including the present, personal, and the critical, judged and distanced. An adventurous aviary of a book.

– Eiléan Ní Chuilleanáin

THE VOLARY

Erin Halliday

THE VOLARY

ARLEN
HOUSE

The Volary

is published in 2019 by

ARLEN HOUSE
42 Grange Abbey Road
Baldoyle
Dublin 13
Ireland
Phone: +353 86 8360236
Email: arlenhouse@gmail.com

978–1–85132–213–8, paperback

International distribution by
SYRACUSE UNIVERSITY PRESS
621 Skytop Road, Suite 110
Syracuse
New York
USA 13244–5290
Phone: 315–443–5534/Fax: 315–443–5545
Email: supress@syr.edu
www.syracuseuniversitypress.syr.edu

© Erin Halliday, 2019

The moral right of the author has been asserted

Typesetting by Arlen House

Cover Artwork: 'Swan, Cygnets & Bogbean' by Poppy Melia
gouache on handmade paper
115 x 51 cm, private collection
www.poppymelia.com

LOTTERY FUNDED

CONTENTS

for my parents, and my parents' parents

My thanks go the following publications, which featured some of these poems, or versions of them:

Banshee, Cyphers, Envoi, Not Very Quiet, Poetry and Audience, Poetry Ireland Review, The SHOp and *The Yellow Nib.*

'Inglis & Co. Ltd.' was shortlisted for the Listowel Writers' Week Irish Poem of the Year at the Irish Book Awards 2018.

I would like to thank Emma Wright for listing 'The Lambert's Day Sermon' as a 2017 Glebe House favourite, and Maria McManus and Paul Maddern for featuring 'Sage-grouse' on the Hour by Hour LGBT Poetry Jukebox in Belfast.

Special thanks to Paula Meehan for the Ireland Chair of Poetry bursary for a 'poet of promise', the Arts Council of Northern Ireland for a generous ACES award, and the Arvon Foundation for a teachers' grant, each of which facilitated the completion of this collection. My gratitude goes, too, to the Tyrone Guthrie Centre at Annaghmakerrig.

I am especially indebted to Nathaniel Joseph McAuley, Damian Smyth, and the 'Old Daffs' poets.

THE VOLARY

THE STOREHOUSE

There were long nutmegs, big matchbox beans
and three-berried candle nuts.
There were ripe banana figs for fig birds,
giant pepper vines for riflebirds and metallic starlings,
clawed-up pear-shaped ivorywood fruit
and Noah's red drooped walnut.

PEAFOWL

My four-year-old self scoring into the sheeny black
layer to reveal the whole pea feather rainbow shell
from the crayon tin; the metrics of fibres colouring-in
the spacings, which would only iridesce if I could crouch,
tilt head, retreat, move in – a courtship of angles
between Kali and Krishna; a lens shift on the coppery gods.

Fifteen mattresses upreared – spring, foam, flock –
yet the tower's as hard as a stone.
I heel and hook myself down to the joists,
drag sofa seat-cushions rafterwise, a hoisted
berth, and, all-fouring it to the porthole,
I grind the latch then slink back to my bedroll rig.
As I'm reeling sleepward, in the dwam, they wriggle in –
sneak-birds, night-birds, not-birds – they scrabble,
swarmy: long-eared, short-headed, free-tailed, whiskered,
leaf-nosed, spear-nosed, sac-winged, pipistrelle.
They yo-yo, parry, make a *wonder room* of the roofspace;
a zoo of velvety peccants shally in dream-orbit, palefaced
lookalikes, horseshoeing in thriftless flight.
The cloud peels away in Dawn's fingery light.

MANDRAKE
after Francis Upritchard, Douglas Hyde Gallery

The pageant troop across the roof: Potato Seller,
Hogweed, Liar, and the rest, follow the leader,
their hand-dyed, hand-tacked smocks and suits
tassled, pinned, or ruched around the neck.
One-by-one, they slip wide chests and jutting shoulders
through the crenels of the battlement.

It's a Moon-day, six hours since spring
as the mannequins – all pied of feet or face,
diamond-faced, pinching frowns –
lower Joan down on a plank; one blue hand straight,
the other, yellow, gathered in.
Hogweed, bunkered like a soldier, says something.

They strut the splines and bights of the lakebank,
leggy rushes – tall as they – shaking their tatty beards
at the dandelion jesters.
White quitch, brittle as old tinsel, scuffs and rasps
as they acrobat across the grass, crook-armed,
thumbs and paint-stained fingers waggling.

Squinting, shrugging, hooked noses twitching,
the motley tribe scrabble about for the dog apple,
till Potato Seller wags his oily cap and Sun Second
tumbles over to jab a lumpy toe at the plum
fruit and lettucey, dock-like leaves.
He raises a straw-long finger to the winds and nods.

Softly, simpery, Liar rummages in the soil,
grubbing three wide circles round the madroot
while Susan, from under her rug shawl, withdraws
knife, wine, speckled pot and fire flint.
Grab lays out the nag poles, fixing the throwing arm
to the mangonel. Allegro plaits nine lengths of hair.

Thumbs in ears, they watch the rod spring back
like a mousetrap, and the hair rope, tied to the crown,
puppeteers the howling nightshade out of the ground.
Ravenous, each scruple of rind and stem is coveted;
the peeled root bark pulped with the knuckle of a twig,
stirred with fingers into wine and boiled till bruise-blue.

Allegro swills a cupful to rub on crampy legs,
Hogweed's juiced the apples, droppers in some nard
and pours the meady tincture in his ears.
The masqueraders slurp and guzzle medicinal
sediment; dopey with weed-liqueur, they trip and pitch
around the mushy kitchen, closed-eyed visionaries.

They turn to Joan and pat the sacramental mash
upon her eyes, plaster salve of Satan's Apple on her scalded
belly, caved-in, cover her – white head to bunching toes.
Her stretcher, like a soggy pyre, is upraised in parade
above their heads, and the holy fools' fête carnivals on
past the lake, led by Mandrake.

CURIO

Longliving Brimstone
first 'butterfly'
crops the Purging Buckthorn
winters on ivy
a brisk flicker
a bright spot of yellow
against snow white evergreens

Should he be concussed
blinded by a glare
in July become too hot
his softness might malign
blotch him red

(aberration *rubescens*)

bleed him olive-black

(aberration *nigrescens*)

With a sudden noise
he may flirt gynandromorphic
one half all male
one half all female

ETYMOLOGY

No *festival*

no *pavilion*

only *a quivering*

and *a beating of the heart.*

THE NATURE RESERVE

The habits and food sources
of the twenty resident species
known by heart.

The shingle flats and lichen carpets
for marsh fritillaries and graylings
transected.

I am not
thought of.

In the Cage Glass

These limbo lifts – my instinct unbuilt
by his rising voice, I waste,
rusted by milky lethargy.

The swagger-man idles
behind me, casts down
his Hellenistic eyes,

becomes just a reflection.

THE NAIADS

Lesson One

Sail a willowherb strand onto the pool.
It ripples close then on, towards, around.

Lesson Two

Lay a pinched cranesbill within the circlet of stones.
It flips in the eddie and spirals out.

Lesson Three

Skitter a mallow flower onto the moss-washed lip.
It flashes, submerges, sun-caught, then surfaces.

Lesson Four

Balance an unopened thistlehead on the flat.
It orbits one current, another, necks round and away.

Lesson Five

Drop a handful of scutch grass in the fizzing white.
It plunges, constellates, lashed there, there, there.

Lesson Six

Float a swatch of lichen by the pebble side.
It rafts dazily, rocks across the rust-coloured basin.

Take the name of the river.
Sing the hymn to Artemis.

THE EIGHTH MONTH

In Liddell & Scott's Lexicon, the word for blossom
and that for carrying make Persephone's festival,

'who was carried off while *gathering flowers*'.

This is the entry after Anthesterion – the eighth month,
'the end of February and beginning of March'.

        o

That was the month I was borne across
from The Ulster to Belfast City Hospital

to begin treatment.

There stands a tree seeded from the one on Kos,
where Hippocrates sat and taught.

        o

The next word, the aorist: '*to lay on* as a burden'
but also 'adding to or *taking away from*

the necessity of death' – like *anathema*, a votive gift.

I found my way to the plane tree from Oncology,
without an offering. My boots got muddied.

        o

Then *antheo* – imperative, *anthein*:
when metaphoric, a sea 'overspread with corpses';

when literal, a disease at its height.

The shortest entry, *anthos* – 'a blossom'.
The plane was fruited with clusters of ripe burrs.

o

An adjective: *'bright-coloured'*, *'fresh, young'*.
23, I stood by the tree, wearing bright clothes.

Passive: *'to be beaten in turn, give way in turn'*.

The penultimate entry – that month,
upon diagnosis, everyone became 'flower bringers'.

o

A final verb – 'to strew with blossoms'.

But if I decline 'bloom' and 'carry' in the feminine
I graft *a girl crowned with petals; a nymph*.

Philyra became the linden, gilded with herby medicinals,
Lotis bore the fruit of wistlessness.

o

Phæthon's sisters wept their sap like oil spilt in the river.

Sidê, rooted in Hades as the red-pulped pomegranate,
was the undoing of that flower-gathering girl.

There was room for ghosting in the untenanted plane;
I tugged loose a leaf from my hair.

INGLIS & CO. LTD.

The streets would be black as bread ovens
    when my grandfather left for work,
the wet flagstones mirrored
    like glassy oysters underfoot.
The house lulled and purring
    in wool, flannelette and flock,
he'd step onto Picardy,
    street lights burnishing the Cregagh route.

Woodstock, over the Lagan, to Eliza Street,
    cobblestones like ostrich eggs underfoot –
or the Belfast Baps he'd watch belted along,
    ceiling height, with their rock-hard crust.
He'd pass the 'day men' at the gates,
    faces burnished by the bakery light, resolute,
then on with his whites – one of the tabernacle:
    Aspinal, Ferris, McCluskey.

Sweet Veda, the powdery Farmhouse, Lodger's barrel
    and Cottage loaf with its garland crust,
the roast and sugared smells climbing the steps
    to the Bread Department; malty, hot –
millers' alchemy: Dennis, Bob, and Jimmy,
    white-shirted, thumbing flour, breathing yeast.
The milky heat would rise, brimming,
    stretch spongey hours on the languid clock.

At home, he'd still hear the kneading gears,
    smell the toasting loaves, watch the clock,
till, 'piece' in his pocket, he'd snib the door
    on the house's purring kitchen in the dark –
from the languid warmth of bedsheets
    to his hours in Inglis' buttery heat;
the streets were black as the bread ovens
    when my grandfather would leave for work.

THE ORGANIST'S MISTAKE

Because he declined to share the praise
with his unseen assistants the bellows-men,
in a great emergency of indignation
the Choir Organ struck loud.

Prayerful daughter of the gallows god, Etheldreda
of Wodan's brood, princess of the Fens –
husband-sister, husband-nun, abbess of Ely –

married the House of Uffingas in the Isle of Eels
to the overlordship. But Ethelthrith,
enskied and prized, fled beyond the Tweed and fenlands

to slip her brashy boy king and the saints of fen-men.
God pitched a tide wall round the vow she made at Elge,
her staff bedded as a nod to her chastity. So Ediltrudis

reared her nuns and veiled the princesses of the island
till sisters and nieces lay down with plague, as Edilthride
said they would, her own neck massy in her fen-side

grave. The quinsey, her due for teenage pride in fenland
gold and turquoise-threaded necklaces, tarnished by eel-side
damp – silver coppered, pearls discoloured. Edeltrude

died of old vanity. The relics of Æthelthryth
were exhumed incorrupt and the hand of the Fen-queen
still outflings cures and wonderworkings in the Isle of Ely.

After twelve visitations the spirit pitched them out of bed. So reports the manuscript – a medieval ghost story amidst notabilia, versus proverbiales, a directorium sacerdotum, hymns, prayers, a litany of the B.V.M. and a list of Winchester benefactors. Initials cradle blue haloed saints; peacocks and holy men peep and lurk amongst the cornflower-and-daisy marginalia and the E of Etheldreda, arced like an oxbow, in carnation red.

Thomas of Ely returned his son to bed, but the vision nodded and the room pealed with recitations of his own prayers, his bodiless oathes on a loop – *amo te super omnia ... tuus gratiam in talem* ... Charmed, dazzled, he followed to her tomb. Barefoot on the sedge and sweet-grass he was bid: admonish the Isle – lax tithes – slack wills – to be put right with ten liturgical parades; an ecclesiastical remedy, prescription for atonement. But Thomas, paupered, bow-legged, was ragged and sulked for a month.

Deus ex machina: Etheldreda squalled across the diocese, 'surge & ambula!' Thomas unbent, as did the See.

Satin spar and isinglass, pearled or snowflake-
patterned, swallow all of the prism colours.
Drusy calcite, paned like an ice rink, cloaks the
spectrum with whiteness.

Sums of light and shadow in voids, inclusions,
interference, cushion or cast back sheen and
lustre as chatoyancy, asterism,
labradorescence.

Specular reflections aventuresce in
sunstone, Goëthite, spectrolite. Opalescent
rainbows flare. Mimicking *Ulysses'* wings the
adularescence

in a moonstone glisters; just like the feathers
of the western lazuli bunting and the
splendid fairy wren as they scatter Tyndall's
ultraviolet blue.

For Childlessness

The Romans had no doubt that the tiny drop of blood
(Pliny says 'a sort of blood': *velut sanguinea*) mid-yolk
in every egg, beat and throbbed. Beat; throb. Beat; throb.
Palpitatque. Palpitatque. Salit palpitatque.

This is the heart of birds: birds' living, birds' wherefore;
the reason for birds.

Test the egg in water. If it floats, it is void – heartless.
Guard any eggs that sink against thunder and the cry
of the hawk by placing a cupful of warm, ploughed earth
under the henhouse straw.

Watch for the new moon, then bring an egg to your bosom
and cherish it in the folds of skin and dresses for nine days;

a heartbeat against a heartbeat –
Palpitatque. Palpitatque. Salit palpitatque.

IMAGO
ut … volitet meus ebrius papilio

Some, small as cardigan buttons,
swooped, snagged,
stunned with a pinch of the chest in the net,
saved, alive
in a glass pillbox till day's end.

But the Dark Blue Tiger,
the Striped Blue Crow,
those that wouldn't fit on your palm,
take the killing bottle
and half a day to soften after.

The delta-blip wing-to-wing reversal
repaired with a puff of breath,
sleeved in glassine,
antennae intact,
Apollo Metalmark, Blue-rayed Metalmark.

Fifteen days rigged
in the relaxing chamber,
basal forewing to dorsum,
zinc-preened,
camphor, peppermint, naphthalene.

Lean in, cheek skimming
chalky wings, mallow-thin,
that twitch as if they could rise
from the pins.
Ixias pyrene, Diorina psecas.

A brittle label, readable
beneath the clearwings.
Not the soul

in the Roman epitaph that flits,
libation-drunk, about the grave.

The Brothers Sleep and Death

Skim down the crest
pendulum in the trough
your fingers curl in
like scorched fronds
your clown eyes
dry and bricked up
the cave of your mouth
full of your tongue
the pain an oily
sandpaper scuff.
Moth wingdust
on the white
of your upturned wrist
a fist's shadow
hoisted above your head.

THE AUGURIES OF BRINDISIUM

A hiss from the blue horned bump
    of the perching bird's bald head
hunched in his rust-coloured mane
    becomes a wheeze, a grizzle.

The knights cage him and his snarling chorus
    and wait for a certain constellation
when they can make a little hollow in the earth
    for bay leaves and blood.

In three weeks, when, small as a rat,
    a wingless dragon twists itself up
from the pit – their birdsong cipher –
    they eat it.

As if a sorcered snake,
    a posset concocted of glossarist flesh
could render the conversation of birds
    native, graspable.

But their ears nonetheless baffle
    at the cowl-bird's kack-kacking
and they tire of its froggy growls,
    its untranslatable buzz.

They trap themselves out in a predawn mist
    to hunt the million-year-old one
with the ferny tail feathers
    shaped like the moon's bow.

Said to speak the human tongue,
    the lyrical bird might impart
the witness of gods that augurs seek to pare,
    that aloft arcana.

Yet all he does caught is mimic
the vulture-headed croak and, deaf
to the sky's riddles still, they serve up
their garrulous, uncribbable catch.

TEMPLE OF THE WINDS

The rain kicked up over Strangford Lough
and he danced for balance in the storm,
photographed the replica water clock-
tower – fine balustrades, fluted columns.
He framed the three-storeyed octagon,
the Scrabo-quarried acanthus leaves,
but he'd never see the bronze Triton
weathervane or full Ionic frieze
lost from the copy of the Acropolis.
The mock temple on the beechwood hill
lacks sundials, is no marble timepiece.
There's no god's shell, stern, basket of hail,
glowing ashes, flower scattering –
each of the eight winds' faces, missing.

CARD XVIII, MAJOR ARCANA

The moon slides the mask to one side,
unfolds ripples on the water
pluming from crawfish gills.
Starlight to sunrise, the cub and pup
loll, swallowing beams.
I tiptoe the hill's snares;
there are yet miles of blue.

WHEN THE SELF RETURNS

to the self, as with the diving birds
to the crested dance –
she recognises the pearl neck feathers,
the blinking eye smile,
the arrow-point crown,
the weed shine in the iris.

IPHIS AND IANTHE
Ovid, Metamorphoses *IX*

Leaving the temple, the spill of her legs bandied –
the tambourines still rattling
and a glow on the altar horns –
Iphis's bright cheeks sagged and grew rough.
Her willowy wrists that bloomed when touched, bulked
and the soft neat spot for kisses in the fold
of her elbow made tough.
The wisps of hair that would lie in the cup
of her collarbone and tickle as they slid
down across the flesh that showed the flush
and pulse when Ianthe came near,
pulled back, short and thick, into her scalp.
Her creamy shoulders spread, stretching her chest
wide and tight and lumpish, no longer rippled
with her feathery sighs.

Venus, Juno, and Hymen came, and caught their breath
and bowed their heads at the easy collect of Isis
– the least of strokes granted.
What would have been a fluid thing,
a sugared thing, hushed, a nest of ravelled limbs,
the girls' wedding night
became Ianthe's arched back smothered and subdued;
laborious and vain, a million times seen –
stallion, bullock, ram – just the momentary weight
of another mounting man.

LAYERING

I would make a Russian doll of us –
you within me, me within you, in turns,
our curved figurines nested tight.

SAGE-GROUSE

The tailbrim spans green sunbeams
in mockery of a carnival: a sage-grass costume
at the carnival of the leks.
The spectators will come from the ridges and swales,
wearing magpie-feather headdresses, skirts of yarrow,
dandelion chains, waving juniper twigs like sticks
of candyfloss – one dressed as a bobcat – and calling
like coyotes all the way to the sagebrush grassland,
or the meadow at the centre of a sagebrush grassland
crowned with a cover of silver sagebrush.

FOR A.M.

Where the bee sucks, there suck I
to watch you streel
amid pewter-grey trees
    and columbines.

In a cowslip's bell I lie
lapping chestnut-sweetened air,
languishing till you appear,
    lorn and moony, shy.

There I couch when owls do cry,
kaleidoscoped in yellow,
as dusk – chalky, mellow –
    burgundies the sky.

On the bat's back do I fly
over green-hemmed fields of bridewort,
cradling my birdcaged heart,
to spend just one night
    cocooned within your sighs.

MILK

I remember
the thought
    she is not mine
when I held her
days old

everyone had left the room
    and I
pushed the teat
    between her sucking lips
to fill her fist-sized gut
with the pumped
    warmed
feed

her long fingers
    pushed and pulled
at the weave
of my collar
her eyes
like a kitten's
    newborn blue
blinking
    closing

I put the bottle down
and cupped her
    a sparrow
both of us
dazed
    dumb

like the room in the farm
with the sow

that
    sweet straw smell
the fleece
of suckling lambs

something
cramped
inside me

she stirred
and turned
    her face
    in
her
pink mouth
    bobbed
and gaped
searched my clothed
    breast

and we
both
ached
for milk

MEMORY'S FIRST HOME

After chemo, Mummy drives by my childhood home
and I voice the names of schoolfriends as we pass.
All is memory, with the glass
taken down from the shopfront of things
so that they can be touched –
the weeds between paving stones
on the long walk back from town.

Lies like balloons are unfastened and bob away –
Christopher and me at playdough
on the seat of my garden swing,
I'd swallowed chewinggum
so I'd die in five days, he said;
the bonfire round the back of our street was Calvary;
Christmas might not come in our new house.

At night, I dream we try the door and it's open.
We move the furniture back as it should be
and swish my bedroom curtains open
on the view down the hill, where memory waits
to be receipted and taken home.

KATSURA

The noiseless heartwood of a tree,
the canopy a flock in the whiteness beyond the lake,
the migration pattern of leaves.

CHRISTMAS WEEK

Alee on the train, I mark a wisp
of amber hairs tacked to the skirt of my thick coat.

One-by-one, or maybe in twos,
the carriage heating current unloosens and sheds them.

I hadn't thought, as I'd stretched my arms
into the quilted sleeves, that I've been wearing this coat

slipping out the back (no bright,
white-whiskered face yawping up by the empty dish),

to sit by your grave. The coat's long enough
to pull the hem between my knees and the soiled wet ground

but last time, I drew the pillow from your makeshift bed
in the garage to kneel on; a seam

of mink-coloured groomings matted mid-fold, which I petted
haltingly. That must've been when the fibres snagged.

The pillow held that snug, dusty smell
I'd crave when I put my lips to the crown of your head;

that intimate gland-smell
nestled in the silky mellow nape behind your ears

that had kept the softness, I'd noticed,
as I cradled you, between the dryer and the stove log stack.

There was no wound. I tweezed leaf tatters
and wood scraps from the underside of your sprawled tail.

By and by, I carried you to Daddy,
to the blackberry patch (I'll plant red cyclamen

between the bay and the 'Forest Flame'),
and wiped some garage-muss from your damp mouth.

Your eyes were open and wouldn't close;
had you woken in the last instant,

seen the moon through the window, dilated?

SHARIPUTRA

Gaping white heron
mind of glowing flowers
dressed in the peace
of remembered lives
neck yawning in flight
emptied of nature
lacy cheeks reddened
in doubling
lit eyes of his mother
pain stained by coupling
made crow black by age
hunching umbrella wings
shading tidal flats
and rice fields
under the Frost Moon
he roosts within
hundred jewelled trees
there is no decrease
there is no increase
there is desire after death.

PYGMALION

This is an art
Which does mend nature – change it rather; but
The art itself is Nature.
The Winter's Tale *IV iv 95–7*

Two boyish girls turn from their ball games
and cloth weaving to ferry the holy parcels
down the hill's tunnel to Aphrodite in the gardens.
Gold-horned heifers slump to the ground
and the flame rises three times, sly.

In the parlour, thick-scented lilies pollened down,
round apples, gold hammered into long-necked swans
and arching dolphins; the sculptor's couch well spread
with Sidonian wool dyed red with salted shells.
There lies the motherless bride, waiting to be thawed.

Mastered, the statue wakes to a kiss, not lucid yet,
and, after the horned orb circles silver nine times,
the warmed skin will stretch and labour,
pall against the heartless goddess's and beauty
waxed by practised fingers will begin to fade.

MANY-WILED
Odyssey *VI*

Dogged and wan Odysseus slept his hard-won sleep
on a wide leaf-litter bed beneath olive leaves –
tattered wild olive leaves – like glowing coal under black ash,

whilst Athene, beamy-eyed, thinking all the while
how she was to bring home her giant-hearted man,
stepped out to get the daughter of Alcinous the king.

On the other side of her lacquered bedroom doors
Nausicaa lay stretched out long-limbed, goddess-faced
on her filigreed bed with two girls – Grace-like – either end

when Athene breezed on in looking sisterly
in her fancy dress as a sailor's girl (one whom
Nausicaa'd known since birth), planting this pillow-side
    word:

'Nausicaa. How can you sleep so easily
with your jewelled shifts and your bright groom's shirts
    bestrewn
around these cushions, sullied? Take them to the washing-
    rocks',

said Athene. 'You are yet unvisited, but
soon you'll marry one of those pretendant lads, and
then your shirts and sashes must twinkle like Selene's'.

The Owl-eyed One withdrawn to the ever bright hill,
soon burnished Dawn awoke the princess, new as she,
who skittled around the palace to find Alcinous,

brave-minded king and father. She saw her mother
at the fire-side, whirling the hand-spun purple threads –
practised – from her arrow-like distaff; waiting-women too.

And there was Alcinous, heading out with his
nobles, gentry, Phaeacian kingsmen, council-bound.
Nausicaa, stepping up close, addressed him lovingly:

'Daddy! Will you get me a wagon so I can
wheel down to the river the piles of my lovely
things that now lie dirty and in need of washing?

You yourself, consorting with princes, surely you
need to dress like royalty — brightly garmented?
And your five sons: shouldn't they sparkle in their dancing
    clothes?'

Mindful of the unmentioned thought of marriage, he
had men bring mules, yoke them to a boxed, hooded cart
stuffed with foods and wine and a golden flask of olive oil.

Nausicaa clopped on her way, companionable,
to the welling river at the pebbly bath-springs
where her maids sloshed armfuls of royal linen clean with
    her.

Chitons and himatia outspread on the baked
shingle, mules unharnessed and grazing, baring their
glossy hair, Nausicaa's girls followed her dancing song –

all outshined by her just as Artemis's nymphs
are eclipsed by glistening-armed Leto's daughter –
as Athene schemed, Nausicaa led them in ball-play.

So Athene, skewing a throw, single-minded
woke the spent Odysseus with a maiden's squeal.
Groaning, played-out, tumbledown, he caught their
    spriteish cheering.

Curious Odysseus, *hiketeria*
branch snapped from his thicket bed, a makeshift loincloth
– modesty of olive leaves – unheroic, all begrimed,

came upon the golden-haired lasses, sallying
like a mountain lion, fiery-eyed, hunger-lorn,
but Athene braced Nausicaa to accept her man.

Chancy Odysseus, keeping his distance, begged
pity – slung ashore by some god, misery-steered –
calling her Zeus's daughter, Leto's daughter, likened her

to the bright palm on Delos he'd once wondered at before.
Happy are her family, he said – three times blessed
father, mother, her brothers; her groom even happier.

Praying for an equal-hearted husband for her,
himself he wanted only to be shown the way,
and this, milk-white Nausicaa, Phaeacian princess,
    pledged.

Calling for her scattered maids to halt, she shamed them:
'This is no trickster – just a luckless wanderer.
Have none of you any faith in high Zeus's protection?'

So, elbowing eachother but obedient,
they showed him to the nearest rill and left for him
the rest of their bathing oil and a clean royal tunic.

This time, the re-arrival of Athene's man,
the guest emerging from his private scrub and dress
with bushy hair curled like petals, was gilded with her
    spell.

Glittering Odysseus settled on the shore,
watched whilst watching, by the princess, imagining,
imagined anchored, heaven-like to her, hers to care for.

He sunk into their lunch things – days since he'd supped on
Calypso's rations. Nausicaa packed the cart,
then hailed him: 'Follow me to my father's palace, stranger.

Walk behind with my handmaids, for our sailors would
deservedly slur me, looking like I'd netted
a husband from the sea, if I ferried you there myself'.

She steered him to Athene's ring of poplar trees,
there to wait until she'd reached home, left directions
to her famous house, there to supplicate Queen Arete.

In the goddess's sacred wood, her shaken man
called out all the names of wily-born Athene,
and she savoured his prayers – about to return to him,

about to return him,
after all,
but not just yet.

The title *The Volary* describes a collection of 'flying things', from the Latin *volo* (*volucer*): 'to fly', 'flying, winged', or the aviary in which they are kept. There are more poems here about 'flying things' – birds, butterflies, bats – than any other subjects, and Pliny the Elder's *Natural History* X and XI are a frequent source. Similarly, Bennie Reilly's 'Rara Avis' series of paintings was the ekphrastic starting-point of this collection.

'Many-wiled' is my approximation of Book VI of Homer's *Odyssey*, in the etymological sense of 'to be near', rather than the line-by-line translation of the Greek with which my process began, but which my reading of the text adapts. Chitons and himatia are forms of ancient garments. *Hiketeria* refers to an olive branch offered with humility by a suppliant.

ABOUT THE AUTHOR

Born in Belfast in 1982, Erin Halliday studied Classics and
English at Queen's University Belfast, gaining her Ph.D at
the Seamus Heaney Centre for Poetry there in 2012. Her
publications are *Chrysalis* (2012) and *Pharmakon* (2015). She
has been a conservation gardener, a university lecturer, a
grammar-school teacher, a creative writing tutor, and now
works in a public library.